My Body
new and selected poems

Also by Joan Larkin

Poetry

Housework (1975)
A Long Sound (1986)
Cold River (1997)
Sor Juana's Love Poems (with Jaime Manrique, 1997)
Boston Piano (Belladonna chapbook, 2003)

Prose

If You Want What We Have (1998)
Glad Day (1998)

Editor

Amazon Poetry (with Elly Bulkin, 1975)
Lesbian Poetry (with Elly Bulkin, 1981)
Gay and Lesbian Poetry in Our Time (with Carl Morse, 1988)
A Woman Like That: Lesbian and Bisexual Writers Tell Their Coming Out Stories (1999)

My Body

new and selected poems

Joan Larkin

Hanging Loose Press
Brooklyn, New York

Published by Hanging Loose Press, 231 Wyckoff Street, Brooklyn, New York, 11217-2208. All rights reserved. No part of this book may be reproduced without the publisher's written permission, except for brief quotations in reviews.

www.hangingloosepress.com

Printed in the United States of America
10 9 8 7 6 5 4 3 2 1

Hanging Loose Press thanks the Literature Program of the New York State Council on the Arts for a grant in support of the publication of this book.

Cover image courtesy of the National Library of Medicine
Cover design by Marie Carter

Library of Congress Cataloging-in-Publication Data available on request.

ISBN: 978-1-931236-74-4 (paper)
ISBN: 978-1-931236-75-1 (cloth)

Produced at The Print Center, Inc. 225 Varick St., New York, NY 10014, a non-profit facility for literary and arts-related publications. (212) 206-8465

CONTENTS

The Offering: new poems

The Offering	13
Processional	14
Testimony	16
Ashes	17
Denis	18
Apprentice	19
A Black Machine Rose	20
Song	21
Kitchen Scene	22
The Bird	23
Jew in Paris	24
Storyville	25
Solo	26
Afterlife	27
Last Seen	28
Heart	29
It	30
The Mask	31
The Combination	32
Backyard	33
Virage	34
Burial	35
Wreath:	
i. Across the Table	36
ii. The Visit	37
iii. Triolet: Nutritional Drink	38
iv. Dirt Route	39
v. Goes On	40
vi. The Atheists	41
vii. Bracelet	42
viii. Phoning My Brother	43
ix. Slow, Over the Granite Stoop	44
Breathing You In	45
Houston to Tucson	46
Inaugural	47

Rouen, 1431   48
Three Songs After Anna Akhmatova   49
Preview   51
Tough-Love Muse   52
Bethlehem   53
A Garden   55

From *Cold River* (1997):

Waste Not   59
Inventory   60
Photo   62
In Time of Plague   63
Sonnet Positive   64
A Review   65
The Fake   67
In the Duchess   68
Beatings   70
Hunger   72
My Body   73
Want   75
To Spirit   76
Journey   77
Here   78
Blue Slipper   79
Cold River   80
Jewish Cemetery, West Roxbury   81
Legacy   82
Robert   83

From *A Long Sound* (1986):

Broken Girl   87
Native Tongue   89
Blood   91
Open Question   92
Fawn Before Bow Season   93
Genealogy   94

Clifton   95
Good-Bye   98
In Western Massachusetts, Sixteen Months Sober   99
Co-Alcoholic   101
Cole's Weekend   102
A Qualification: Pat H.   104
Self-Doubt   106
Origins   107
Rape   108
Blackout Sonnets   110
Ring   114
Cow's Skull with Calico Roses   115
Struck   117
Alba   118
Hard Differences   119
How the Healing Takes Place   120

From *Housework* (1975):

Rhyme of My Inheritance   125
Secret Song   127
Housework   128
Song   130
Story   132
Work Song   133
The Women's School   134
8th Street: the Aquarium   135
Direct Address   136
Song of What I Wanted   137
The Fire   138
Some Unsaid Things   139
Stop   140
"Vagina" Sonnet   142
The Bombed Villages   143

for Kate Aguilar

THE OFFERING: NEW POEMS

THE OFFERING

When they cleaned you and gave you to me,
long legs and fingers, red glow
rising from creased flesh,
eyes already awake, gaze steady,
I shook for three days
in my knot of hospital sheets.

Tears came later—
cries, fears, fierce holding.
The ways you'd shake me off.
Your well of rage. Over and over
you bloomed in your separate knowledge.

Yesterday, you offered tender words.
I remembered gorging on *teglach* Fanny made,
thick knots of dough shining with honey.
I'm filled and wanting more—only to taste
that heavy gold on my tongue again.

PROCESSIONAL

In Tamilnadu
where it's still morning,
where the mixed scent of
burning rubber, incense
and excrement hasn't yet
heated to a thing you sweat
through your feet and tongue,
where day is beginning to burn
through the neem leaves,
a long string of men
snakes along a dirt route, chanting
and in their center like a gold bead
lofted on their shoulders
a man sits in a painted box
its canopy dyed bright yellow
and he, too, is clothed yellow
and his face upturned to the sun
is smeared with turmeric:
a man the color of saffron grain.
He's leaning back in his high seat
and you see from your safe distance
his stiff posture and open mouth.
You stare as if you've never seen the dead:
Francis in his smeared bedding,
your father a waxwork
freakish in mortuary rouge,
all the young men in varnished coffins.
Each death its own strangeness,
a gold face tilted to the light.
Yet common to all. You're
in this moving line. And he is,
the one you carry, the one you praise

and want to spare.
The line jolts forward
Jaya, jaya, Shiva Shambho
toward the wood and fire,
and you breathe the scent
of everything alive.

Testimony

I wasn't the only drunk reaching
for Kleenex as short Arnold
on the foot-high platform
choked the wild sound
rising in his throat. He was filled
and pouring joy like anguish.
Tears drew light to his face.
Two hundred of us in the room
and none coughed or shuffled
or scraped a metal chair
as he said how he saw
clear sky spreading above him
and a thing like a lead band
that snapped and freed his chest.
I didn't drift for once or argue
or make lists for later.
I let the hush wrap me,
felt how John was near me,
Steve across the big room.
I saw how Mary lifted her chin,
how Sybil suffered in her bloated flesh,
her unreadable lipstick smile.
For a moment all was as it should be.
Everyone in the room knew it.
I think so. It wasn't some dream.
Harsh blues, heads nodding
amen — not even that. How
to explain it. I wish you'd been there.

ASHES

I thought they'd be fine and white
as beach sand in a glossy ad
for the good life, honeymoon-cruise
sand, so I was shocked by grit
that was your bones un-
consumed by 1500 degrees of heat
and flecked like the sand at Brighton,
where once I dragged a nice Boston girl
to show her the Moscou, the greasy
kasha knishes, the Polar Bear Club—
old, hairy Russians plunging into icy
brine—a Sunday ruined
and now forgotten, long after the day
I waited in the upstate police station
to sign for your body. If there was a crime
it was your sudden dying, of which I was
innocent, though the cop's grimace
behind the high counter haunts me.
I was often in the wrong then
and thought he could see
how I wouldn't grieve, how I'd stall
for months before I picked up your ashes.
We cast you into the Hudson
you loved and praised with heavy paint,
and what was left of your
drunk anger and lovely flushed
skin, your terse, barely audible wit
and dark flame of Irish hair
was gone, everything burned, sifted,
dropped into the cold, slow current.

DENIS

when you were grass in the wind
when you were a silent wave
when you wallowed in blood in the midst of the highway
when you shed out your bowels to the ground
when you were a friend of silence
when you were a cloud
when you fattened like a caterpillar
when you crossed the braided stream on stones
when you offered yourself at the rest stop
when you lit up the house with white candles
when you were afraid, alone in the metal bed
when you came back as God's roar in a dream
when you took the mouthful of bitter fluid
when you were new
when you crowed and whispered
when you lay on your back looking up through blue-black fruit
when you were a fool
when devils devoured your reason
when you were a lord of truth
when you chose the moss-slick stone, the knobbed branch
when you held the lamb's skull in your cupped palm
when you were beyond our praise
when you climbed the black rock rising out of the Atlantic
when we climbed after you, wanting a last photograph

APPRENTICE

I must have been five or six
when we lived in Everett during the War:
Donald could identify every plane
and collected scrap in an old carriage
for we were patriotic
and *Bubbe* darkened the kitchen, rehearsing
for air raids. Winter then was like this one,
always night,
and thick sooty ice hid the sidewalk,
and I'd go down to the cellar
behind Dad — I was the one
who stood and watched while he loaded the shovel
and aimed black chunks at the fiery
mouth. He let me try it —
didn't he? Don't I remember the weight
of the wooden shovel, the weight of coal
picked from that heap without light
under the chute. And if he did say
You do it, then that was the moment
I first tried lifting my father's
burden, taking on his work, climbing
down steep wooden steps
to feed the thing that was always there
in the dark with its mouth open.

A BLACK MACHINE ROSE

A black machine rose
high off the wooden desk
upstairs at the Chelsea Olympia
where he worked in his 30's—
wide tie, middle part,
mute eyes, sniper
wit I didn't know yet.
Lifted me onto his lap:
Go ahead. I pressed
the Royal's round keys
& ink bit paper.

SONG

It wasn't written down—you
banged it out from memory.
It's nowhere in this pile of books
I'm excavating for a shard
of pocked green porcelain,
a pack of Luckies, a good pen,
for the sight of you
standing by the bathroom sink
with a folded towel,
fake eye in your palm
the glistening almost-twin
of the living one.
This time I'd look straight
at the pit where they dug out
the ninety-nine percent.
I wouldn't be ashamed to speak.
When you said *I can still
drive*, I'd reach for your
free hand and hold it.
If I saw you propped, smiling,
with jaundice-gold skin,
instead of sneaking somewhere to smoke
I'd say *Thank you. Thank you.*
Do you miss those nights at the piano?
You crashing the keys with
huge paws, pulling wild honey
from a broken hive.
Roaring your song at me
so you don't have to sing alone.

KITCHEN SCENE

Her I lost years ago, but I have this
picture, I can't lose it, I'm standing here
in the kitchen doorway back from school,
bookworm dying to go read in the deep chair
& feed on sneaked cookies. She's kneeling
on wet linoleum, stockings rolled, red
hand throttling a brush as it streaks the floor
with ammonia suds. She won't look
where I'm standing inches from her raised arm,
but as if alone, lit, onstage, she howls *I hate*
my life, I hate my life! Her sobs ululate
in time to her violent scrubbing. But it's no opera.
Her voice my embryo despair, I'm sobbing, too —
Mama, Mama, please — what did I do?

THE BIRD

Betty Florence May Joan, she called me
all of her sisters' names first then landed
on mine — often summoned me thus, warbled
the arpeggio of names in her alto register,
though I can call up only the once — Florida,
I'm rounding the white sofa, she cries
her song of names from the kitchen, she's not
falling, no, no, she's moving on her own steam,
feeds the cockatiel, baiting her bottom lip
with torn toast, and the goldgreen bird, out
of its cage, perched on the ceiling fan, squawks,
swoops, grabs the treat from her mouth. *See! See!*
her voice is gleeful. I nod, I want to be reading,
I'm scarcely looking, Celia, what a great trick,
how do you do it, and even now that she's in the ground
fourteen years, cold Massachusetts, I can't look for long
at her pale eyes, her hands tearing toast, her years of days
alone with the humid kitchen, the canny bird.

Jew In Paris

How did my 92-year-old aunt
find me here? Flo, the pretty one.
In the tattered album she's a slim flapper
in belted knits cut to attract a Gatsby.
Religion didn't take over until
she gave birth to two rabbis — already
speaking slow syllables in the womb,
tightening *teffilin* around their foreheads.
I'm still the offending speck of *chometz*
they find by candlelight and flick
from the spines of prayerbooks, the crumb
of leavened bread that defiles Pesach —
they burn it the morning after the search.
Shame of the family, dead ringer
for my blond, goyish father. Gleefully
eating *quiche au jambon*. Passing.
My aunt's looking through me into
this case of silver circumcision knives
and bowls for catching blood and foreskins.
Dense, hand-inked script
in medieval leather-bound books,
silk hats, ritual shawls
only for men, salvaged gravestones.
I'm walking my dead, heavy flesh.
On the first floor, they've hung banners,
cloth replicas of *cartes d'identité*
of those wakened by loud knocking,
who were dragged, strangled,
shot over ditches onto snow muck.
Some without love for religion. *See*,
says my aunt. *Names of our tribe*.
And now the knocking begins in my body.

STORYVILLE

Boston 1956

The three of us sat at a round table
afloat in lush smoke-haze
drinking metallic orange juice and gin
the waitress hadn't refused us
high-school kids faking boredom
me in heels and lipstick David in dark
wool Lanny frowning tightly and I
was on my second drink watching
dust spiral down a shaft of light
the room a velvet tunnel
as Ella in a black gown landed exactly
on each note of From This Moment On
my skin buzzing as the boys' crewcuts
bobbed in tempo and I hoped I'd reach
home before my parents. This was before
my shame and violation before Lanny
tried to eviscerate himself with scissors
and David's dense weave of notes landed
him too in a gold spotlight and none of us knew
they'd raze the place and build a high rise
so I breathed smoke and shining brass
and sweat and "you for me, dear"
in my untouched skin practicing
to know everything, to get this
drink down fast and order another.

SOLO

The drive, Boston to Newport,
in slanting rain, the plastic tent,
beer in a plastic cup, my ruined
dress, soaked hair, the solo
horn ripping bottom to top,
its cheerful impatient shriek
poised between schlock and paradise
never heard on any record,
the long trip back, the feeble heater —
me shivering while Harvey Smith,
odd duck of Cambridge, Mass.,
pored over his map by flashlight,
the night truly over when I heard
how my father had watched through the window
and thought he knew what he'd seen
as I argued with Harvey, engine running,
then walked up solo, 3:00 a.m., to be punished
when all I'd done this time
was ride hours in numbing rain
one whole New England state from home
and sneak into my father's house
after I'd clapped for Louis Armstrong
live, in the flesh, not even knowing
the half of what I was hearing.

AFTERLIFE

I'm older than my father when he turned
bright gold and left his body with its used-up liver
in the Faulkner Hospital, Jamaica Plain. I don't
believe in the afterlife, don't know where he is
now his flesh has finished rotting from his long
bones in the Jewish Cemetery — he could be the only
convert under those rows and rows of headstones.
Once, washing dishes in a narrow kitchen
I heard him whistling behind me. My nape froze.
Nothing like this has happened since. But this morning
we were on a plane to Virginia together. I was 17,
pregnant and scared. *Abortion* was waiting,
my aunt's guest bed soaked with blood, my mother
screaming — and he was saying *Kids get into trouble* —
I'm getting it now: this was forgiveness.
I think if he'd lived he'd have changed and grown
but what would he have made of my flood of words
after he'd said in a low voice as the plane
descended to Richmond in clean daylight
and the stewardess walked between the rows
in her neat skirt and tucked-in blouse
Don't ever tell this to anyone.

Last Seen

On empty pavement
under infected elms

by houses lined up silent
windows admitting nothing

no spendthrift peonies
no dropped dolls

to worry the guiltless
borders of short grass

that time I came walking
and froze to see you walking

through dead quiet
and freezing light

my body marked for cutting
and yours just beginning

you rebuking and I
shrinking into the harsh story

which for all I know
still serves you

wherever you moved and married
and had your reasons

and after what we did
undid my body's reason

I was scraped to a small word
as they took saws to the trees

HEART

His is honeycombed, each hexagonal cell
sequestered, walled in kryptonite, a solo
gold-lit compartment, no view of the others.
Look, you can open one door at a time,
it's an Advent calendar of little rooms.
His wife's in this one, angrily buzzing
over her small horde of honey. In this one
his mother reigns, rich in the hope of Glory,
still holding his baby picture as an offering
and praising Christ. In this one, his violin,
his clear tenor—hymns, pop tunes, Mozart—
this one can sing and sing if only you open it.
Don't forget the one with his folded uniform,
Scout's honor, straight-A report cards,
or this one: loss held in solution
like amber, hardening toward no future.
And look—there *you* are, still in a plush
box all to yourself. You're the best of the lot,
you think—or at least still delectable when thought of.
If you stir even a little, he'll open the door.

IT

It was right in the middle of my back,
smooth, I thought black, shiny,
twisting to see it. Hard to the touch,
I thought metal. Size of those little snails
out back on the vine leaves, raised,
round. I couldn't stop trying
to touch it—you know, the spot you can almost reach
between the vertebrae. It was embedded,
it wouldn't budge. Where it fused with the skin
the skin shrank, puckered around it.
I squeezed my shoulder blades to dislodge it
and maybe it moved a little.
Woke knowing it was there. Scraped
against doors, crouched at the sink edge
and yanked upward—all that did was score
the skin next to it. Raw for a week,
new stain on the cotton whenever I checked.
Talked to myself in the kitchen,
Learn to live with it.
I don't think they can see, though it
must have showed through the thick
sweaters and jackets I took to wearing then.
I got used to it, what choice did I have?
I carried it. That was how it was.

THE MASK

Your face
in light filtered from the street
lay tilted against my arm.
We were backward now,
heads at the foot of the bed,
and as we stared into each other, smiling,
your face was a cartoon by Daumier,
a death's-head, an I-don't-know:
eyes smaller than I'd known
and round,
mouth a carved opening:
eyeholes, mouth-hole in a taut mask
all there was of you —
and was it you?
white clay or jade or Olmec stone
I couldn't say.
I looked, and looked away.
I stared —
it was the same.
The face stared back, smiling.
I closed my eyes
and pressed into you,
and then we were those two again —
I think we were —
just resting animals again
stretched out together, after the hot feast.

THE COMBINATION

Silent, Dot heaves herself onto the bed,
eyes, hips, and pale, heavy breasts
lit by the stuttering bodega candle —
Rembrandt's Saskia, except for her set mouth.
Neither of us has done this sober much.
Terror's running neck and neck with desire
and neither finds relief in simple touch.
Face on face, lip pressed against lid,
hands blunt on breasts, minds gone numb,
we work the combination, spring the lock
and rush for home still hoping to find
her there, the one who suckled us in the old myth.
The bed groans. Dot rolls away half smiling.
Well, she says. We got *that* over with.

BACKYARD

Call it the camel's straw, how she hoisted her sledgehammer,
smashed my cement walk, then swore she forgot
I'd said — twice — *Leave it intact.* I'm still
picking up chunks of broken cement crusted
with earth, snails, stones. I don't grudge
her force or fury, the wrecked path. What bugged me
then was her innocent *Oh. I forgot.* Christ,
what if she'd cried *Cunt, I wanted to kill you.*
She'd be some other woman then. She'd know
such words — no, not words but horror buried
under the rock, the monster mother
you hack to bloody chunks, sink deep in the yard
and still her hair and ragged nails thrive, forcing
their blameless way up into the light.

VIRAGE

What was I thinking of, showing off
my ten-year-old Swedish car, parked
outside the same wannabe French
bistro where tonight, *seule,* I'm eating
grilled lamb between teaching and movie,
remembering — *Christ!* — this was the place,
April, I offered to pay
her check, and her head on that pale
stem of a neck turned side to side, refusing.
She was back from the West, this time with nothing
to brag about after an avalanche of calls
to ex-editors, students, lovers,
her sudden German accent — *Their drugs
are poison, I'm not safe, oh please. . . .*
But that was over, her face was a swept
room, she was sober, proofreading nights
and looking for work — though what could she do,
computers had raced past her, and I
stood with her on Sixth saying *Me, too* —
hollow small talk — *Isn't it awful* —
as if I knew, thinking I'd call her,
maybe we'd even get back together,
as if she weren't already planning
how, in the borrowed bedroom she showed me
around the corner on Eighth Street
murmuring *I'm so lucky, lucky,*
she'd rest her slender neck in a belt,
two weeks after that ignorant meal.

BURIAL

The lush perfumes of that day,
explosions of birdsong, dogwoods opening
jewel-pink by the groomed path —
you'd have written it as Hell:
the tame priest reading the standard prayers
in his young, public voice —
the words *sister, lamb, sinner*
standing guard over deleted facts
as awkward sunlight hurt us.
You'd have nailed the numb factions:
brother, cousins, muffled in good wool,
your death to them as shameful as your life;
your friends in dark glasses, kneeling
in wronged silence, placing bunched flowers;
your bowed father, his grief
an irony to those who blamed him.
I want to think you'd have spared none of us,
your acid stripping the morning
down to its lethal contradictions —
I think that's how you'd have written it —
if only you'd been there.

WREATH

i. ACROSS THE TABLE

Cheeks flaming, puffed by prednisone,
entirely deaf now, braying,
Ann calls Donald a bad man —
how can the cat stand to look at him?
Yesterday she called him a saint.

I print on the pad DONALD'S TELLING ME THE STORY OF HOW YOU
      MET KAI KOBAYASHI.
Her eyes widen. She wails
Poor Kei and *Wasn't that the worst, worst* —
all through the heavy dessert.

Watching my brother's taut ambiguous face,
I think I do see the saint —
not smiling at torment God allows —
but holding his old life —
a cracked cup
holding everything,
not spilling a drop.

ii. THE VISIT

He mixes stuffing from a box,
feeds the animals first —
my dog makes eleven.
Says *I get confused if anyone helps*.

Comes when Ann yells for him.
I print on the pad, HE'S COOKING.
He comes anyway.
Sweetie.

Ann reads captions on the silent TV.
Tells us *Those Islamic caves*
where I heard Hillary Clinton singing —
I sang with her.

Bowed, he slowly fills three plates.
Dust everywhere, cat hair on the piano lid —
magazines slide to the floor and he says
Leave them.

iii. TRIOLET: NUTRITIONAL DRINK

As long as he sits beside her
holding a straw to her lips
his life has purpose: *provider*
as long as he sits beside her.
And she is his provider
though most of the liquid drips
down her chin as he sits beside her
holding the straw to her lips.

iv. DIRT ROUTE

Slow, slow. The wipers only spread
the mud and road-salt splatter. This is Swanville,
no fishing through new ice yet, though
every year some fool drowns in his SUV.
Left at the failed dairy farm, uphill
past Freedom Motors — shut. No one.
Sharp right at Bridge Closed sign.
Steep drop. I watch for frozen ruts
all down Steele Road. No
light in the house, but from behind
the door the faint familiar barking.
Road of no mercy, let me leave before dark.

v. GOES ON

Dried blood on the table under the heap of *Newsweek*s,
water standing in the plugged sink,
crusted dish, white with a blue border.
We say *Work will save him*,
say *Thank God for the animals*.
Cat on the fridge stares at the screeching cockatiel.
Dog claws again at the gnawed door.

vi. THE ATHEISTS

I surprised myself calling the priest Father.
He was 5' 5", thin hair combed slant.
He leaned on the syllable *us* in *Jesus*
and smiled and nodded through the tapes I played,
Ave Verum Corpus and the dead woman singing a lullaby.
And Donald took the brass cross that had touched her coffin
and hung it above his bed for comfort,
choking tears of shame as he told me.

vii. BRACELET

My brother moves from room to room, pile to pile.
He's kept everything—
sweater still wrapped in plastic,
chairs spilling sour laundry,
jumble of stretch pants, outsize tops
you could force over her head sunk on her breast.
Drip-dry flower prints—
cheap raiment of her end.
Moccasins curled to the shape of her feet.
Did she walk on her own
or was the social worker correct,
that he bore all her weight?
Bathroom tray of dusty costume jewelry:
she sat there twisting rings on and off.
Some, dropped into the bowl, were lost.
I should have taken the estate-sale bracelet he offered—
to take *anything* away.

I thought he might need it—

viii. PHONING MY BROTHER

This Sunday devotion —
a service I'm rendering?
But I need his voice
to see him: stooped,
standing on ripped linoleum,
adding to a pan of leftovers
while the cats twist
through towers of cans on the table.

He shuts off the rice — always a talker,
any question will start the mudslide
of facts and opinions. This time
the true key of a Chopin prelude
some idiot transposed and what
the gifted doctor who was also a tuba player
said of the piece Donald wrote for him:
trickier than colon surgery . . .

how he's kept the oil bill down,
and now that the ground's thawing,
the date of Ann's interment is set.
No need for you to come this far:
I see him standing by her raw grave
as the priest intones the short service.
I don't want to bother anyone —
says this without weeping —
to the sister waiting to hang up.

ix. Slow, Over the Granite Stoop

Sciatic nerve a rope of fire,
he turns, latches the warped door.
Ignores the trapped stench —
he keeps his windows shut on purpose.

I drag a chair, angle it to face his way.
Watch white stubble on his moving jaw.
And breathe, from the brittle wreath,
December's clean, astringent balsam.

Breathing You In

The scent you say is no scent
rises from warm ports
between neck and shoulder.
Scent that isn't witch hazel, vetiver, camphor, lemon,
but is just your skin,
raises a breeze on mine, unpredicted
as freshness I found in woods
where a few blond leaves hung from twigs.
Sweet sharpness,
scent of something still to come,
something soaked in —
chlorine on the cedar deck your thigh presses,
foot drifting in water,
eyes yellow amber behind closed lids.
Soaked in like sun
in the river whose cold silk
wrapped your body in August,
opened dark folds around you.
Closed, opened, around you.

Houston to Tucson

So heaven is fire, too:
these lakes of flame — gilt-edged —
and below, a cerulean stream
draws us, steady over alps
of whipped curds. How
can she read her magazine, or he
fill his crossword, ball pen
stalled in the pinpoint gleam —
am I the only child
cheek pressed to pane
as hell's pilot
ferries us through heaven?

INAUGURAL

We started in the dark,
four crammed into the green Ford,
its rack-and-pinion steering bad
so we hawed in the wind
as we passed our bag of apples
and sang our way to DC
the day of his anointing.
Joined the human stream winding
around the stone courthouse —
supremely empty. No one opened a hose,
no one fired rubber bullets,
for this was democracy — we walked,
hoarse and sodden, lifting up signs and puppets
for one another all day in raw January rain —
and saw many passing the other way
in black Stetsons, in minks draped to the pavement.
They sneered as they walked past in their boots,
faces smooth and satisfied.
The bullies' feast was beginning.

ROUEN, 1431

Once, as I lay in their filthy cell, pants laced
tight under my tunic, both knees
drawn to my breast — that was how I slept —
the guard's mouth gone slack, I rode
his snorting breath back to Les Tourelles.
Smelled gunpowder, felt it exploding
with sharp cracks, heard the wounded screaming
as I helped raise a scaling-ladder
against the redoubt, above us small axes,
maces, naked fists, yet my men climbing.
I was armored in full plate, except my head,
and the English archer found his mark between
my neck and shoulder. His arrow pierced
my flesh to its depth and came out
through my back. Its force flung me backward.
In the dream I was afraid again and wept,
Catherine not yet with me, as they stuffed
my wound with cotton, olive oil, bacon grease —
no anodyne. The pain came back to me
and almost woke me, and I saw the judges'
seals, thick red wax hardening on their paper,
before I saw Her light and heard Her voice.

THREE SONGS AFTER ANNA AKHMATOVA

Now no one will want songs.
The days they said would come are here.
Listen, song, there won't be any miracles.
Don't break my heart. Learn not to sing.

You can't be the bird you were,
your risky flight, your full throat.
Get used to hunger. You'll be a beggar
knocking on strangers' doors.

—1917

Why is this century the worst?
Dazed with grief and dread
it's sunk its hands into our stinking wounds
and healed nothing.

In the West, the sun's sinking
and roofs gleam in the late light.
But here, Death chalks doors with crosses
and calls the crows, and the crows are coming.

—1919

To Death

You'll come anyway, so why not now?
The night is bitter, and I'm waiting.
I've turned off the light, left the door open
for you — so simple, so fabulous
you can take any shape you like,
a gas pellet, a strangler —
or why not infect me with typhus?
Or come as a character from your own Grimm's tale,
the one we're sick of hearing
where you stand in the door
behind the blue police cap
and the concierge shitting with fear.
I don't care how you do it. The Yenisei
is churning, the North Star is glittering,
and my beloved's eyes
are dark with the final horror.

— 1939

PREVIEW

Dread of morning and of evening.
Wind a faint hiss,
a wave dragged back across stones.
Blood-moon. Swarm of flies.
Cicada burning a wire through brutal air.

Will we whisper what we know
or bet on silence
or learn to praise the butcher god
while dogs slaver
and loudspeakers go berserk

Tough-Love Muse

Praise grief all you want,
More loss is coming.

You think history's cruel;
There'll be worse damage.

Don't sit down with the stupid,
They're going to want to eat.

Forget the one who threw your songs away —
You won't run short of *schmaltz*.

Can you find a sliver of soap,
Comb what's left of your hair?

Lace your shoe?
Stand up?

Then leave the museum and let
Dust lie on old, fine things.

Breathe in again.
Again. Please

Don't tell me you can't
Sing.

BETHLEHEM

My arms and legs were dark as earth
from picking—small olives knocked
from the gnarled trees then pressed
into oil, then grapes, then pomegranates
till rain poured in torrents down the wadis.
Fifteen and pregnant, I left my mother's house,
her row of jars, stone for grinding,
quick hands turning out loaves.
I rode behind him. They were counting
us like sheep and cows to tax us.
The dust stung, but I felt my strength
rising—I could have harvested vineyards,
pressed the wine. Then inside me a jar
broke and warm liquid drenched my thighs.
The innkeeper's wife looked me over shrewdly
and pointed us to the mud-brick shed in back.
I lay on the threshing floor and waited between
the clenchings—dull cramps like menses.
I drank some barley water he brought me. A girl
led in the cows and the shed breathed with their big bodies.
The girl gave me water to clean myself—that was when
I saw my arms dark against my belly.
The cramps came faster, the furrow was widening,
then the bursting pain of the baby's head
as it tore the opening. I squatted over strewn chaff,
tensed my thighs and pushed, waited and pushed,
and as I thrust him out in a rush of blood and water
I smelled the cattle and my own pungent smell
and felt the damp cold on my clotted
hair and shaking legs. I was not
tired. I had never felt such pleasure
in my house of flesh. In that moment and in

the hours after, cord knotted and cut,
baby cleaned of blood and bound in cotton,
nothing they'd ever told me mattered. His mouth
found my breast and pressed from it the first liquid
that comes before milk and I pressed him against me,
earth feeding earth. Later I laid him to sleep in straw
in a feeding trough — they'd sold one of their cattle —
and lay down next to him as night streamed through
the open doorway. There were no shepherds yet,
no magicians no gifts no ideas — only his body
and my body, flesh joyful and shivering.

A GARDEN

We were planting in black earth
the last night of my life.
Death was scheduled for morning.
I was happy, planting lilacs now.
She wondered, *Too many?*
& I laughed, it was rich. I said
you never can have enough lilacs,
look at New England. I dug
on the low roof: this one
would spill downward.
The dream, November,
was drenched lilac. Life
was this plenty: earth, lilacs,
the woman next to me planting—
I hardly felt any fear
this morning, shaking.

From *Cold River*, 1997

Waste Not

We're using every bit of your death.
We're making a vise of your mouth's clenching and loosening,
an engine of your labored breathing,
a furnace of your wide-open eyes.

We've reduced you to stock, fed you to the crowd,
banked the pearl of your last anger,
stored the honey of your last smile.

Nothing's left in your mirror,
nothing's floating on your high ceiling.
We're combing pockets, turning sleeves,
shaking out bone and ash,
stripping you down to desire.

Your beloved has folded your house into his —
I'm wading the swift river, balancing on stones.

INVENTORY

One who lifted his arms with joy, first time across the finish line
    at the New York marathon, six months later a skeleton
    falling from threshold to threshold, shit streaming from
    his diaper,
one who walked with a stick, wore a well-cut suit to the opera,
    to poetry readings, to mass, who wrote the best long poem
    of his life at Roosevelt Hospital and read it on television,
one who went to 35 funerals in 12 months,
one who said *I'm sick of all you AIDS widows*,
one who lost both her sisters,
one who said *I'm not sure that what he and I do is safe, but we're
    young, I don't think we'll get sick*,
one who dying said *They came for me in their boat, they want me
    on it, and I told them Not tonight, I'm staying here with James*,
one who went to Mexico for Laetrile,
one who went to California for Compound Q,
one who went to Germany for extract of Venus' flytrap,
one who went to France for humane treatment,
one who chanted, holding hands in a circle,
one who ate vegetables, who looked in a mirror and said
    I forgive you,
one who refused to see his mother,
one who refused to speak to his brother,
one who refused to let a priest enter his room,
one who did the best paintings of his life and went home from
    his opening in a taxi with twenty kinds of flowers,
one who moved to San Francisco and lived two more years,
one who married his lover and died next day,
one who said *I'm entirely filled with anger*,
one who said *I don't have AIDS, I have something else*,
one with night sweats, nausea, fever, who worked as a nurse,

one who kept on studying to be a priest,
one who kept on photographing famous women,
one who kept on writing vicious reviews,
one who kept going to AA meetings till he couldn't walk,
one whose son came just once to the hospital,
one whose mother said *This is God's judgment*,
one whose father held him when he was frightened,
one whose minister said *Beth and her lover of twelve years were
        devoted as Ruth and Naomi*,
one whose clothes were thrown in the street, beautiful shirts and ties
        a neighbor picked from the garbage and handed out at a party,
one who said *This room is a fucking prison*,
one who said *They're so nice to me here*,
one who cut my hair and said *My legs bother me*,
one who couldn't stand, who said *I like those earrings*,
one with a tube in his chest, who asked *What are you eating?*
one who said *How's your writing? Are you moving to the
        mountains?* who said *I hope you get rich.*
One who said *Death is transition*,
one who was doing new work, entirely filled with anger,
one who wanted to live till his birthday, and did.

PHOTO

A winter afternoon lengthens on your pillow.
Head propped, hair fanned out around your forehead,
dark lesions on the bridge of your nose,
you're lying back, loose hospital gown
a blizzard of blue snow. Eyes bluer.
Your mouth open in a smile or grimace,
not yet vomiting blood like rich black
oil from the well of your animal self.
Not yet the open mouth I saw in a photo like this one —
Peter Hujar newly dead, face of a Mexican Christ. You
are alive, and it's still your mouth, Francis,
framed by your new beard —
soft, sexual — I could put my fingers through it.
A shock of chest hair lies
across the loose skin of your throat,
creased flesh he kissed who laid his cheek there,
tongue along your breastbone tasting your salt.
But death is in progress —
your slow, arduous climb; its rude surprises:
blood, shit, vomit, in rooms full of friends;
falling, forgetting;
your lost rhythms of sex and running;
your long body a mask for bone.
I'm looking at your photo, Francis —
it took three years.
You, looking at your death.
Your powerful, candid eyes.

In Time of Plague

When you sit with me I forget
how thin you looked, waiting,
like a boy in shorts; how the dark
look crossed your face,
an eclipse casting its flank of shadow.
We're sitting in light, smiling,
me saying, *Odd not to live here now.*
You, *If I get sick —*
You leave your fish uneaten,
rake kale with your fork.
Your polite *If* — I seize it,
break my roll in pieces
as you paint a future hell
where you're helpless against our pity.
I stop eating, hard seed
lodged in my tender gum,
everything in me looking
at you as your face tilts up.
I can't believe you've left the city!
Blood heats my face,
my spine feels cold.
I'd come back — I pray
to mean it. You don't
contradict me; you smile, swallow
water. I notice the young
waiter's full, dark hair,
the sweet, slightly rotten
smell of freesia, as
we look away from each other.

SONNET POSITIVE

Nothing is life-or-death in this slow drive
to Vermont on back roads—lunch, a quick look
at antiques—though he does bring up his grave
and wanting a stone. The road curves; we joke
about the quickest way to ship ashes
to England and whether he ought to have
himself stuffed, instead, like a bird. He flashes
me a glance that says it's ok, we can laugh
at this death that won't arrive for a while. We pull
over. He's not actually sick yet, he reminds me,
reaching for the next pill. His bag's full
of plastic medicine bottles, his body
of side effects, as he stoops to look at a low
table whose thin, perfect legs perch on snow.

A REVIEW

It wasn't the worst movie
I've seen about AIDS.
Lots of nice family.
Catholics who never flinch
from kissing their infected son.
Nobody saying Do you mind
not holding the baby,
not even the pregnant sister
says I love you, but I can't let you
inject yourself in our house.
Not once does the father cry
Where did we go wrong?
Red ribbon looped in every lapel,
no one afraid their faggot
son will burn for eternity.
No one too queer,
no one crazed from death
after death. No kissing,
nothing scarier than a glimpse
of KS sores like a map
of new islands under
the hero's immaculate shirt.
He's a boyscout who once had sex
in a porn theatre, went there
three times in his life —
no 900 numbers,
subway toilets, sadism,
anger, failure, complexity —
it's a movie, isn't it?
How could I expect him
not to die the minute he says
I'm ready — no weeks

of morphine & oxygen, whispers
at the bedside all night,
exhausted laughter, pleading:
You've got to leave your body;
there's nothing left for it but pain.
It was a six-dollar entertainment,
popcorn spilled in the aisles.
But somewhere in the middle, a scene
in a library. The unshaven
gaunt face, the cheap
watch cap, were yours, Denis.
I saw you staring, stripped
to your fear and wanting to live.
And later, listening to Callas,
the dying man's lifted face
flickering green, red—
pleasure, dementia. Love,
it was your face, & I wept.

THE FAKE

The man in front of me is you
from the back — the same
wrinkled plaid, the same
fine hair, wire rims.
When he turns, I see
his red face — a coarse
copy of your lost health.
The room is hot.
I scan the crowd
for anyone who knew you.

IN THE DUCHESS

Sheridan Square, 1973

Women swayed together
on that scuffed floor. I stared
at the strong beauty who stood

and shook her tambourine.
The poised waitress poured,
hips pressed against hips —

I drank their half-closed
eyes, half-opened lips,
link bracelets, ease

of illegal dancing. Soon
I'd cut my hair, soon
sharpen cuffs and creases,

burn bold as the stone
butch staring back
in whose smile my fear

and wanting found a mirror.
There, amid booze, smoke,
loud unmerciful music,

my whole body was praying
that now my real life —
molting animal,

new, wet skin —
would come touch me
and, at last, I'd dance.

BEATINGS

They beat me different ways.
My mother was standing
in her light summer suit and hat.
She was late; it was my fault.
She was almost sobbing. A cord
was twisted around her breath,
an animal trying to escape
from her throat. Her knuckles landed
hard on my shoulders, in my ribs and guts.
Her face was close. She was yelling,
yanking me by the hair, and I saw my brother
standing near us in the hall, watching.
Standing and forgetting why he was there
watching and what he liked about it.

I was younger. I think we were all there,
four or five in the kitchen, father home
for supper between shifts. He lifted me
over his knees to hit me. Belt,
brush, or his large hand came down
open and steady on both buttocks, burning
and stinging through thin underpants,
big voice in control, saying This
is for your own good, This
hurts us, This is because we love you.
I cannot remember my crime, only my face
against his knees. His hands, his strong
voice telling me I was loved.

When the man beat me later
in the bed in Brooklyn, the kind man
with big lips and hands, the man

who loved me and beat me
with the same voice, when years later
in the same bed, the thin woman with tattooed
wrists told me I couldn't receive
love, thrusting the dildo till I was
sore and crying *Stop*, she laughing,
shouting I couldn't love her —
it wasn't true. I loved the rising
of their voices — his dark, steady one,
sure, in control, and her demented one
rising like my dead mother's wild voice.

HUNGER

Turned on. Turned off.
I was both, as she smeared the lube
the way you'd spread margarine —
flat hand, quick upturning wrist —
she was a worker.
I was a cut loaf. I was a client
from her child whore time.
I lay thinking how her first sex
was "to get it over with quick
so I could work" — as her mother worked,
as they worked together and alone
learning the quarter where a man
could feed you or kill you.
Her hand on me was firm, a boxer's,
her body narrow, dark, hard.
How ludicrous a cock and harness had seemed before this.
I wanted it and didn't
as she snaked up the bed —
leather, flesh, sweat shining,
eyes like an animal's
staring into me as if she had a right —
that cat I'd watched her seize with both hands
and shake, gazing at its face
and shouting *I love you!*
We lay slant,
mouth on mouth, breast on breast,
clapped together, ringing.
She pressed into me so hard
I could feel my ribs and the bones of my face,
I could feel her impossible hunger.
In the end,
I too arched and reared.

My Body

Throat puckered like crepe,
right hand throbbing with arthritis,
right hip permanently higher than left, right leg shorter
after years of books slung from one shoulder.
One breast smaller, both sagging like Grandma's,
      shriveled around the nipples,
upper arms lumpy, veins in legs varicose,
back freckled from sunburn when I passed out on the beach
      in 1964,
face creasing, still breaking out, hairs bristling from bumps
      I didn't start out with,
nose pitted, burst capillaries on nostrils,
two extra holes pierced in the left ear so I'll never forget
      those months with Sido—thank God I refused the tattoo,
two vaccination scars,
shoulder stiff from fracture in 1986 when I fell on a stone
      floor at Cummington,
skin dotted with—what? moles? age spots? melanoma that
      killed my father?
sagging belly, testament to fear, dieting, birth, abortion,
      miscarriage,
years of fighting booze and overeating still written in my flesh,
small cysts around labia, sparse pubes—not yet like my head
full of grey that first appeared the year I had two jobs and
      pneumonia.
Eyes needing bifocals now, no good for driving at night,
still blue and intense, tired but my best feature—
or maybe it's my hands, strong, blunt, with prominent veins.
Lungs still wheezing after years of asthma and smoking,
all of me still full of groans, sighs, tears,
still responsive to the slightest touch,
grief and desire still with me

though I hardly ever have reason to close the curtains,
naked fool for passion —
and wonder if I'll live alone the rest of my time in this body —
my old friend now,
healed and healed again,
still walking and breathing,
scars faded as thin silver signatures.

WANT

She wants a house full of cups and the ghosts
of last century's lesbians; I want a spotless
apartment, a fast computer. She wants a woodstove,
three cords of ash, an axe; I want
a clean gas flame. She wants a row of jars:
oats, coriander, thick green oil;
I want nothing to store. She wants pomanders,
linens, baby quilts, scrapbooks. She wants Wellesley
reunions. I want gleaming floorboards, the river's
reflection. She wants shrimp and sweat and salt;
she wants chocolate. I want a raku bowl,
steam rising from rice. She wants goats,
chickens, children. Feeding and weeping. I want
wind from the river freshening cleared rooms.
She wants birthdays, theaters, flags, peonies.
I want words like lasers. She wants a mother's
tenderness. Touch ancient as the river.
I want a woman's wit swift as a lynx.
She's in her city, meeting
her deadline; I'm in my mill village out late
with the dog, listening to the pinging wind bells, thinking
of the twelve years of wanting, apart and together.
We've kissed all weekend; we want
to drive the hundred miles and try it again.

To Spirit

. . . God of breathing,
I pray that my mother will make her breakfast and really eat it,
that she will wash herself and walk to the kitchen without falling,
that my brother will shut up about the nursing home,
that she will dress herself in mint and pink polyester,
pay her rent,
take heart medicine,
sleep through the night,
read a book again.

That her friend Sandy will bring soup,
that Mary Hoyt will sit with her,
Marian shop for her,
Meals on Wheels feed her.
That nightmare will not harrow her,
no man frighten her,
my brother not bully her, bully her.

God, do not abandon us in our age
or worse, let condescending children control us.
For choice is the life spirit in her
even as she becomes a child.

And as work is taken from us,
and as home is taken from us,
and as sex is taken from us,
and as the body is taken from us,
and writing is taken
and the mind lightens
and we are divested even of sense —
let Self remain —
and choose —
Spirit, all praise to You —
choose, even on the last day.

JOURNEY

Her bedroom's sour-smelling, hot; the pad
backed with electric-blue plastic, drowned.

She's hunched and grimacing. I'm going home
on the next flight; I smile back, don't

dare be afraid. I ask, How was your night?
I got up once, to go—that's all. Her exhausted

bright eyes are a child's. *Next time,*
I want you to bring me Kate. Her cane's on the floor;

she reaches for it, grabs the nightstand, lifts.
Steadies herself on walls, doorknob, TV.

Staggers. Achieves her end:
the pink bathroom.

HERE

I breathe with her:
the long nothing, then the gasp.
I want to rest between those groans,
those blank stares.
Rest my cheek against her freckled arm,
my face in the cool L of her elbow
watching her neck tense and relax:
half minutes, her mouth sunk open.
I want this to stop.
Look the length of her body,
length of her pale life,
all hollows and soft mounds;
below the pulled-up gown, sparse net of hairs.
Her eyes are closed, she's quiet.
The not breathing lasts less than a minute.
She groans. Then, *Joan!*
Where have you been all afternoon?
Here, I say.

BLUE SLIPPER

Nothing in this day —
not the doe this morning
looking uphill through my windshield
so still I thought she was light;
not the young priest, saying
The place to pray from is God's heart —
I went there a moment when he said it;
not even the road inked with pines,
bright shawl of fog,
hills the color of deep water —
nothing in this world, Mother,
is poised in my mind like the blue slipper
that won't fit your swollen foot.
Good terrycloth scuffs from J. Byron's
I don't think you saw. They came in a clear
plastic envelope. I opened it for you,
wrote your name on the soles with a black
marker. The nurse said *You might as well
throw them away.* Over a year now
I can't get it on you, Mother,
can't get it off.

COLD RIVER

My mother disappeared in a shoddy
pine coffin in the rain
while my brother complained of its cheapness
and one aunt whispered
as I took my turn shoveling
in black clothes and shame.
Before that, she disappeared
in a useless body we fed,
lifted, tortured, four months.
Suddenly the house was full
of thin, rose-painted china.
The valuable ring she'd kept
where they couldn't steal it
felt loose on my middle finger.
The day I phoned from Shelburne,
the nurse whispered to me,
Now her legs are weeping.
I was resting from her long dying.
Mother, I said. *I'm in the cabin.*
I can hear you — twice
she dragged words to the surface.
I can't forget that voice.
It was my first. The bitter
edge I hated as I grew wild
was the only weapon of the woman
who called me *Daughter.*
Now it's a current in me
like the cold river
I take grief swimming in.

Jewish Cemetery, West Roxbury

Inside the city, a city of stone slabs,
acorns dropping on mossed walks.
I find hers at the far end in a walled corner,
a grave bought in the '40s, before the crowds.
I am happy and kneel,
not thinking about the rain
last summer when they opened
the deep trough for her.
Not thinking about her feet
nor my own frozen months.
My working lungs are a wonder to me.
Whatever is left
of flesh, shroud, box
can't hear me,
so I speak openly to the day,
mouth tender with praise
as hers once she forgave me.
I find three muddy stones
to leave in honor of life's hardness.
A beetle forages among them
as I walk to the car
beneath the gift of a daytime moon.

LEGACY

When my mother finally left her body
it was mine to keep
along with her ring,
some blackened silver,
a box of Jewish books.
At first I thought it would be a difficult fit
but here a tuck and there a seam let out
and you'd swear it was made for me.
My freckled throat,
creased stomach,
soft, white hips—
even my thoughts at 3:00 a.m. are hers.
I'm lying here in her body!
She doesn't miss it,
she likes the way I look in it,
winks when I feed it her favorites.
Sunday I'll walk down the aisle at my daughter's wedding
and the thin breasts in grey silk
will be my mother's. Veins in sticky hose,
bunioned feet in shoes that match the dress—
more and more will be hers.
I'll walk past the narrow eyes of those who doubt me
safe in my mother's armor—
faux-pearl choker and stiff, glittering clasp—
as their whispers weave around me
my face wearing her little smile,
her scared eyes shining in triumph.

ROBERT

Right now in Fayetteville
where it's two, not three o'clock,
you're doing what you did then:
driving a rattletrap, maybe
on a road lush with spring green,
or sharpening a Venus drawing pencil
by a river that's slowly drying out.
I see the thin green pencil,
not the hand holding it —
I can't remember your hands.
There's a dog with you, not
the one we had together —
she must be dead ten years.
I see you in worn flannel
and round gold glasses. Those
must be gone, too,
with the hat I hated,
the square brown one with earflaps.
I want to call you on the phone.
Want us in Tucson together, 1962,
before my father died. Before
any of it. I want to be kind this time,
and not just to you.
I want my mother back,
the way she was then:
not thin or grey yet,
not sweet the way she was later,
starting to die. Robert, she forgave me:
for divorcing you, even for writing
that I was queer. She didn't say
she forgave me, she just said,
Oh well, you turned out all right.

I want to call you
in Fayetteville, right now,
so you can say it too: *I love you,*
in your surprising baritone.
I want to say, *Mother,*
please sit with me in the orange kitchen.
I have something to tell you.

FROM *A LONG SOUND*, 1986

Broken Girl

seconal and wine   I lived on the street
I slept wherever night found me
abandoned buildings   boxes   always
it wants more from you
it wants you
to drink
it doesn't mind if you die
I didn't mind

there came a night I had nothing
I went on a roof to kill myself
I prayed first   You
make the decision   let me die
or live
a long sound
Wa. . .   the sound of life
entered my body like a breath

held me   it was warm
a bell hung in my heart
a bell of feeling
glowed in me
then the silence   peace
it was then I got sober
after a vision you have to do it
so the next one can come to you

I want you to know this
sometimes I think I won't make it
yesterday voices were singing
kill yourself   this
goes on for years after the drugs

right now I'm alive   grateful
if you find it hard to believe
look at me

NATIVE TONGUE

My first language was wet
and merging
My syllables were not distinct
from hers; our liquid interface
floated my slow vowels
in the infradark
of her hold,

my serious fish   face
my belly with its tendril
registering her depth
charges.

My first language was light
split by white slats
into molten series
buzzing with dust —
light on my dry, new body.

Vaseline,
clean worm on mama's finger
on my vulva
while I lay, white diaper, white
chenille spread, legs across the edge
of the big bed.

My first language was food:
thin, warm thread of milk
dull oatmeal in a pewter bowl,
gingerbread — round boys with raisin eyes,
grandma smiling, standing at the iron stove
with its porcelain cocks and nipples.

The dog's breathing and the dog's dry tongue —
she was and was not a person.
Dirty they said, but told
how she was Celia's
good girl.
Her high bark
sliced thin portions of the cold.
She was my size.

I was smaller than the steep words
around me: tommy gun, stolen,
hitler. Mother is a nurse's
aide, father is an air raid warden
in the dark cellar. His helmet
is white and important.

We are jews. There are bombs,
oil, an icebox, a victory
garden. You can count by twos
in your hand with fat green seeds.

BLOOD

You mix flesh, your first time with his paintbox:
raw sienna, white, a squeeze of red.
His knife spreads grease rainbows on the palette.
What will you do, now that your father's dead —

you of my poems, whose eyes swallow me
whole, like the dark that drank Persephone —
you spread the paint with delicate bloody strokes
on a large redlipped woman you say is me.

You ripened in my blood like a red fruit
until you split the air with your separate breath.
Then I could not protect you from the fathers;
nor can I bear for you now this father's death.

We paint each other large: daughter, mother,
images delivered of each other's dark.
I've drunk the light of your hair. You've swallowed hell
and can survive the ways it wants you back.

OPEN QUESTION

In your curved house
(take care of, take care),
as the tender column of your neck
turned, as you slept
(take care) —
still unsolved,

was your soul scraped free
of your body *(take care)*
like the last jot
of dependent flesh
the curette freed
from my clinging womb?

Fawn Before Bow Season

The day I went to work,
I stopped nursing you, I pushed
the thick rubber nipple between your lips.
Something in your eyes' dark lakes
disappeared—did I really see this?
Daily you were drenching ten pounds
of diapers, bedclothes. You weighed
nothing. Puffball.
I held you in the crook of one arm.
Your small breath warmed me.
Work at the computer billing company
began at nine. The sitter could give you
bottles. When I was done
paying her, there was money
for one week's food—
I knew this was true,
even when Jim said, *That job
costs you more than you take home.*

Tonight,
end of August, you are eighteen.
I'm fine, you repeat on the phone.
There's a cool edge to the air,
the season turning. It's dusk.
From my open car window, I see
the fawn, head lifted, half
over the fence. For a moment,
she moors me in her dark gaze—
then floats back, soundless,
somewhere I can't see.
Nothing I know can hold her in the field.

GENEALOGY

I come from alcohol.
I was set down in it like a spark in gas.
I lay down dumb with it, I let it erase what it liked.
I played house with it, let it dress me, undress me.
I exulted, I excused.
I married it. And where it went, I went.
I gave birth to it.
I nursed, I plotted murder with it.
I laid its table, paid its promises.
I lived with it wherever it liked to live:
in the kitchen, under the bed, at the coin laundry,
out by the swings, in the back seat of the car,
at the trashed Thanksgiving table.
I sat with it in the blear of TV.
I sat where it glittered, carmine,
where it burned in a blunt glass,
where it stood in a glittering lineup on the bar.
I saw it in the dull mirror, making up my face,
in the weekend silence,
in the smashed dish, in the slammed car door,
in the dead husband, the love.
Alcohol in the torn journal.
Alcohol in the void mirror.
My generations are of alcohol
and all that I could ever hope to bear.

CLIFTON

I loved booze,
and booze and pills I loved more.
I still love them.
I still want them.
My wine, my Dexamil,
my after-dinner tall
tumbler of Scotch,
my morning black espresso,
my Valium at work,
and more Valium.
It worked.
The Dexamil let me drink,
the drink kept me from feeling,
the Valium kept my hand from shaking.
The Dexamil let me drink
in the face of my psychiatrist saying,
I think you drink too much —
I think I won't see you if you drink.
In the face of fines,
in the face of swinging at a cop,
in the face of connecting with a two-by-four,
in the face of cops looking down at me in the middle
    of Amsterdam Avenue
in a Brooks Brothers suit, a briefcase,
in the *middle* of Amsterdam Avenue —
Where do you live, sir? We think you should go home.

I drank at Hanratty's for four reasons:
it's near where I live,
they cashed my checks,
they closed at one,
and they took me home.

At home, I would have another
Scotch and a pill,
at 5:30 get up,
drink coffee, take a pill —
I had — I have —
a responsible job.
I was always first at my desk
and last to leave.
I never wanted to work.
I wanted someone else to take care of it all.

I don't know why I'm alive today.
I don't believe in God, I'm a strict Freudian.
When I stopped, I thought,
This is unspeakable deprivation.
I whined and cried.
I sat in the back eleven months
pitying myself. Home
from a dinner with board members,
with two glasses of wine, the first in a year —
I opened the half bottle of Scotch
a guest had left. It was months under the sink.
Often I'd thought of it. Always,
I knew it was there.
I poured Scotch into a tumbler,
and I couldn't drink it.
I couldn't. I thought, *I can't go through all that again.*

That was ten years ago.
My hair is gray. A doorman
with whom I left a package yesterday
described me to my friend as "distinguished."
Lots of things are the same.
Some things are changed, changing.
I love booze in my dreams.

I drink booze and take pills in my dreams.
I don't ask *Why*
do I love alcohol? Instead,
I have habits strict as the former ones,
meetings, books, service.
The dreams full of booze keep telling me what I am.

Late in my life,
in the numb elegance of this city,
I made a decision —
or the decision
shining in the soft, brutal darkness
took hold of me —
to live.
Often I am peaceful.
I never imagined that.

GOOD-BYE

You are saying good-bye to your last
drink. There is no lover
like her: bourbon, big gem
in your palm and steep
fiery blade in your throat,
deadeye down. None like her
but her sister, first
gin, like your first
seaswim, first woman
whose brine took to your tongue,
who could change the seasons of your cells
like nothing else.
Unless it was wine, finally
your only companion, winking
across the table, hinting
in her rubies, her first-class labels,
of her peasant blood
and the coarse way she would open you.

Good-bye, beauties. You don't want to say it.
You try to remember
the night you fell out of the car
and crawled to the curb, the night
two of you stood
screaming over your daughter's crib.
You remember deaths
by gin, by easy capsules —
the friend who fell in silence
and the friend who quoted *Antony* in his suicide note.
All this helps for a moment, till your heart
blooms and stiffens with desire.

In Western Massachusetts, Sixteen Months Sober

*The first year I was out here, because there were no
flowers, I began picking up bones.*
—Georgia O'Keeffe

To find words for this.

There's a tree. And its shadow.
And a wind washing the shadow
uphill through the weeds.

Once you said to me,
There's a word for everything.
Words
I don't trust now.

I'm walking uphill—
no fiction.

Phrasebook of a country I'm visiting.
I remember the names from before.
Goldenrod, cricket. The cedar waxwing.
Driving downhill, a couple. Backseat, the kids.
The field blows toward me hard.

The late light chooses
white stones in the wall,
a white moth, and the white leaf
turning.

To simplify—
I tore so many papers.

Briefly
it was winter. Then
in Brooklyn, at the bottom of my house,
someone in the mirror
wearing my plaid robe,
still asking to be carried.

Walking home, the low sun
on my bare arms.
Outside the blind piano tuner's house
air stirs the flag,
a pony trots,
a boy watches his sister.

Francis, a year ago you asked,
Do you have the willingness to be happy?
I can't always say.
Today
I'm climbing this hill,
I'm picking up
this pen.

Co-Alcoholic

I saw you in the street, head lowered, stumbling;
I waited two years to call.
This is the last time, I told myself.
Unless he's dead, I'll tell him about the fellowship.
This time, no ice against glass against my ear —
"I'm sober," you said.

You were trembling, pallid,
your fat a cradle around you,
the old tattoo like a bruise purpling your arm.
You kept trying to kiss me.
"I need someone I don't have to impress," you said.
Should. Shouldn't. I judged myself without pity.

You remembered 1969, an acid trip,
the *I Ching* hexagram we'd formed, fucking.
Above, the clinging, fire; below, wind and wood.
Lake over fire: molting, an animal's pelt.
Last night, the rose and bruise-purple of my cunt
were the colors in my mind's eye

of slick internal shapes twisting and coupling,
Blake's underworld river, looped like a gut.
Above, the abysmal, water,
below, the receptive, earth —
hair glistening like oil
on your thin chest my breasts wilted on.
Last night the fear in my eyes stared at the fear in your eyes.

COLE'S WEEKEND

I came down from Lowell to see Brad.
I was working late shifts alone,
no one to speak to, machines
slick and dangerous. Staying
at my parents' again, like velvet handcuffs.
I borrowed the silver Skylark.
I remember me the

blond, twenties, eyes
clouded over, face
like dough left standing, gray.
Did I think anything?

I parked. I got there
just as the weekend drinking
was getting off the ground.
I think they were glad to see me.

I remember bits. Vodka,
lots of it. Some musical
I passed out in. Brad's dad
patting my shoulder in a downtown
bar, buying us
boilermakers. Joan and Brad
in that lurid light, leaving us,
leaving me Joan's keys —
which I lost. Me trying to scale
their building at four a.m.,
coming to on the subway tracks,
head resting on the wood
guard for the third rail,
me on the train, getting a whiff

of my pissed pants, my bloodied hair,
no jacket, no car keys, no license, no memory
of where the car was.

We drank
what was left of Sunday.
Brad's father had my jacket, keys,
i.d.—everything was great!
Except that I'd missed work
and was out of money
and my body had several bruises,
I wasn't sure where from.

The weekend was over.
One minute
I was in the left lane on the Mass Pike,
next thing I was drifting toward the guardrail.

It wasn't going to be easy
getting home.

A Qualification: Pat H.

I talked to the bathtub.
It was made of atoms;
atoms were alive, I reasoned,
so the tub was alive —
it was my friend.
Sometimes I fell into it.
Oh but I didn't bathe —
I stank in those days.
I talked to it for hours,
also to the Barbra Streisand poster on the door.
I'd sit facing it —
my six-pack next to me in the sink —
drinking, pissing, for hours.
At least then I wasn't pissing on *her*
or in those goddamn shorts.
It's a miracle I'm here to tell you this:
all those years I tried to be dead.

One doctor said I was premenstrual,
one diagnosed grand mal epilepsy
and let me go. *I'm sick!*
I thought, and got some vodka down.
One day I sat looking at the glass in my hand
and I knew. It was that sudden.
Something wanted to live;
it wasn't me.
How the message got through
my fog   my denial
I can't tell you.
There has to be a higher power.
Still, no instant change.
I fought recovery.

I had one slip five years ago
and tried to kill myself.
It was when my mother died —
I won't go into it.
It's different now.

It hurts to say all this.
I need you. Talk to me.
How does my life remind you of your own?

SELF-DOUBT

The sky cracks along
a branch of sycamore: its fault.
The sidewalk, split in jigsaw-
puzzle pieces by the roots,
lifts, oblique to itself.
The foreground—leaves and bark—
collapses like a sinkhole
while the sky's crazed blue
bulges like heavy crockery.
Everything seems to have two
sides. I could be wrong.

ORIGINS

It was a party; I had on my party dress.
There was something wrong in Grandpa's friend's throat.
I kept him waiting outside the bathroom
while I read *Mother West Wind "When" Stories.*
When Mama yelled at me to *Make it fast,*
I wiped. I flushed. I came out on the landing
holding the blue book behind my back.
His lighted cigar was the red eye of an animal.
He reached a hand up — big, spotted like an animal —
under the short skirt of my party dress.
I felt pleasure, and I felt afraid of the hand.
Nice girl, he was smiling,
and the red eye shook and smelled like a cigar.
This was at the top of some stairs —
what house was it?
Were there stairs on Westminster Avenue?
How little was I? I remember. Little.
I said, *Mama, the man touched me.*
No, she said. She was worried
about the party; she was serving
a tray of green things and pink things.
She explained the facts to me quickly.
No, she said.
The man is a nice old man.

Rape

After twenty years I want to call it that, but was it?
I mean
it wasn't all his fault, I mean
wasn't I out there on 8th Street,
wandering around looking for someone to fill the gap where my
     center would have been?
Didn't I circle the same block over & over until he saw me?
Wasn't I crying when he came along & said *Don't do that, cops see me
     with a white girl crying —*
I'm sorry. Didn't I say *I'm sorry*, & didn't I smile?
Didn't I walk with him, dumb, to the Hotel Earle,
didn't I drink with him in his room,
didn't I undress myself in the stare of a yellow bulb?
Didn't I drink — what was it I drank?
Didn't I drink enough to be numb for a long time?
Didn't I drink myself into a blackout?

Was it rape, if when I lay there letting him fuck me I started to feel
sore & exhausted & said *Stop*,
first softly, then screaming
Stop, over & over?
And if he was too drunk to hear me,
or if he heard me but thought, *Girls never mean it when they say stop*
was that rape? Was it rape if he meant well
or was too drunk to hear me, was it rape
if he kept repeating *Girl, you can fuck*
& not really meaning any harm?

I think I remember that the room was green & black,
the small bulb dangling from a cord,
the bed filthy.
I don't exactly remember.

I know I had no pleasure, but lay there; I don't think he forced me.
It was just that he wouldn't stop when I asked him to.
He didn't take my money.
It may have been his booze I drank.
It may have been sort of a date.
He wrote his number on half a matchbook & said
Call Joe if you need him — I guess he was Joe.

Did I walk home?
Did I have any money?
Was it me who bought the booze?
Maybe I took a cab.
Was it 2:00 a.m., or safe daylight
when I climbed the five flights,
spent, feeling the tear tracks and pounded cervix,
the booze still coating me, my nerves not yet awake, stripped &
            screaming.
I climbed to my place, five flights,
somehow satisfied,
somehow made real by the pain.

Was it rape, then?

BLACKOUT SONNETS

Something happened I couldn't have told you then.
He was dark, with a beak like Uncle Ben's,
another salesman in a suit. Barry, my music teacher's son —
a senior, hot when I was twelve, Book One
propped on the instrument.
Now I was eighteen. My mother was intent
about my hem and hair. On her knees,
mouth full of pins, she spit out sharp advice:
Don't overdo the makeup. Face
facts: you've got my hips. She was amazed
a plausible, tall Jew would date
her daughter. I was damaged goods. Too late
to do me any good, she'd said last year,
You're nothing, if you've lost your precious treasure.

❉

You're nothing, if you've lost your precious treasure.
So I guess I gave him nothing, on the sofa
in his parents' finished basement (big TV,
plush carpet, bar) listening, New Year's Eve,
to his favorite Gershwin — which we had to hear
twice. Zero degrees, I felt numb about the year
1957. His folks, a blur
of blue cigar smoke and a full-length fur,
were climbing into the Caddy as we drove in.
Goodnight — I was unprepared. She still looked grim
as when I hadn't practiced, which was most
of the time. Barry, the conscientious host,
opened two bottles of sparkling Cold Duck
one after the other — the suave fuck.

One after the other, the suave fuck
followed the fake champagne. I wasn't struck
by the way I took his cues; only his taste
appalled me. Eighteen, I was a wine-snob, based
on one date with a transfer student from Paris.
Cold Duck fluorescent in my blood, black dress
hiked to my hips, my pale pink synthetic
panties spilled on the rug, his tireless prick
battering my numbed entrance — I couldn't say
whether or not I wanted it that way.
For all I know, we would have gone someplace —
dancing, a movie — if, in my half-a-voice,
I'd said, *No more, thanks*. Or *What are your plans?*
Whichever, I was in his hands.

✾

Whichever, I was in his hands —
what shit. I wanted him inside my pants.
I knew my lines and hurried through them. Once
drunk, I could direct him, no coy hints,
to close the coffin and then nail me in —
that was the point. Fucking put a lid on pain
like nothing since the rubber cone of ether
on my nose and mouth that night last year.
Saline injection, hot curette in my womb,
blood in the toilet, mother screaming in my room —
the whole damned family was in on it.
Brother, cousin — all of them suffered the secret.
Now Barry flickered and passed out.
Had either of us come? I was in a blackout.

✾

Had either of us come? I was in a blackout.
It was two when I woke up in the Buick on Route
Nine. I stared at the immaculate floor,
carpeted to match dark maroon leather
upholstery. My high heels pierced the shag.
I fished inside my black patent bag
for keys and hoped my mother was in bed.
Barry drove without turning his head.
My pants were soaked. I shivered, though the heat
was blasting. Queasy — *We didn't even eat* —
I clung to my cold keys and stared at signs
and Barry's profile, trying to read his mind.
And in a tone he might have meant to soften,
he said, *Do you do this sort of thing often?*

❖

He said, *Do you do this sort of thing often?*
No — I could barely say it. My face stiffened.
It sickens me even now, remembering this:
I had been hoping for a goodnight kiss.
Skidding on new snow, the Buick turned
my corner. Barry clammed up. The cold burned
as he opened the door on my side, courteous,
distant: he had had nothing to do with this.
I grabbed his cashmere sleeve and climbed the icy
steps to the squat brick house I
hated; my folks had moved here right
after the abortion. September, a soft night,
Uncle's knife scraped out my next-of-kin.
Now I drank anything and slept with everyone.

❖

I drank anything and slept with everyone
and kept my mouth shut about the abortion.
I hardly remember 1957 —
I stopped speaking to my closest friend
when her boyfriend called me up and said, *I want
your doctor's name.* His sleeve soft, my cunt
sore, we climbed the stairs to 7-B.
Mom opened the door and stared at me
as if I were a mirror. Was my dress
zipped only part way up? Barry glanced at us,
looking supremely sane, said a smooth *Goodnight,*
and left. Her laugh a snort, *You're good and late!*
she said, and *Will he ask you out again?* —
and something happened I couldn't have told you then.

RING

It was late, it was just before work —
and I thought I had lost my mother's
ring! Running from room
to room, I thought of all
I had lost: I broke my mother's
cut-glass dish, unraveled
her patient afghan — endless
worm from one pink
string — the things I had ruined!
Sloven, I let the dog in,
left the garbage boiling
with maggots, the gas on, the plugged-in
iron heating the house.
Engines idled everywhere I turned
keys. Meters were ticking,
taps bleeding, The kettle
screeched. The house
was flooding, stuffing itself
with steam. In the cellar, oil
was inching, fattening the stone floor
into loam. As I ran from bedroom
to bathroom to bedroom, facing
the blind drawers, the grinning
drain, floorboards wincing
and crying, the tall house
was thickening like spores
in your throat once you eat
the death cup, white
Amanita. The taste exploding
in my pink mouth, *You're dead*,
my friend, I said to myself,
and, too late,
found it just where I set it down.

Cow's Skull with Calico Roses

Nothing soft in this skull
hung up, somewhere —
so it appears in this print
though to be painted
it must have been laid on cloths.
The black split between two continents
of white linen
could be O'Keeffe's table.

Sheets — softly folded
petals of flesh —
or abstraction:
white labia
or a white cello
fretted with thick silk stems
of a calico rose
concealing the cow's jawbone.

It's hard to see things
as they are said not to be,
but harder
not to see the cross
imposed on this flat sheet,
the split in this
tradition of painted space
she chooses.

She takes West to its limit
in this picture. Bleached
needlework flowers
hint of women's hands,

hot afternoons.
Hard not to see
the farmhouse, white
blister on the land.

Christ could be in this,
or the painter's faith
in desert light.
But I see an abortion —
papers torn to bits
with words on them —
a body fretted
by an unlike nature.

A disappearance, an abyss —
in this skull shaped like a pelvis
cracked in the center,
the black vertical plummeting
into a calico spiral,
the unlikely collaboration
of things to outlast a life:
its artifacts and bones.

STRUCK

You got me scared right off the bat
with your saying you'd like me to buy this house
& you'd had a hot love affair with a strong woman —
a quick confession. You're as reckless as I am.
You say you love me, you're happy I'm here. You say, Come
spend the summer; I may go to Minnesota though.
On my own so fast! I think, staring at the tadpoles —
there are thousands wriggling in this little lake
with everything in it, near it, above it, stirring
fin, wing, tail. I rub the dog, you rub my leg, we talk
& groom ourselves like seals against each other.
Your thoughts shock me like last night's lightning
striking right by the house. The house rolls
& your cups in the kitchen's thunder peal as they fall.

ALBA

Weeping, I twist awake, won't tell you what:
a pink fizz drink I didn't want,
wet pants, my frozen tongue, my wasted brother. . . .
You hold me in your sleep's surface tension
until the buzzer rips you from my text.

No laughs allowed as you groan, *I forgot my toothbrush*,
swiveling into jeans that mean business.
The past is past: pitch of my cry, coming,
that keyed your nerves' flash flood at 3:00 a.m.

Later, it could snow. Now you go out, in the pink
first light of a clean borough. Through a clear pane,
All Saints cuts the white sky like cake,
that cloud's a dragon snorkeling through the spires.
Cold angels watch you—there's a gull—and bless.

Hard Differences

Your face
like a map of mountains

your body
creviced, blushing
with its dark areoles

Aetna, Vesuvius . . .
Monadnock —
something volcanic and Latin
crashes against my Massachusetts rock

or the opposite

my lust
pilgrim to your stone
Roman-emperor heart
moated by oceans

How the Healing Takes Place

How the face changes, the cloud
you'd skim from a pot of lentils
comes clear, how the gaze
comes clear as honey when you heat it,
how the eyes surrender their fear,
dark lake of beach plums
boiled for jam. How flesh

yields new flesh, lips
softening like soaked beans.
How the puffed skin settles,
dough becomes bread,
its brown, delicate grain.
How the dead hair — that mouse,
matted and stiff in the trap —
grows sleek again. How the thoughts,

like black ants going
and coming from the mouse's corpse,
go slower. How the torn mind
puts forth tendrils.
How the gray house of the lungs,
frayed and weather-beaten,
fills with moist breath.
How the breath brings healing

to all parts of the body.
To the salt rivers of blood,
to the many-tiered skeleton,
to the breast, beaded and creased,
humming like wings in the jewelweed,

to the softening belly,
to the thick, unfurling petals of the sex.

How everything speaks —
hands unclenching —
heart.
How the belly will lift its flat
stone, the tears roll
stones from entrances.

FROM *HOUSEWORK*, 1975

Rhyme of My Inheritance

My mother gave me a bitter tongue.
My father gave me a turned back.
My grandmother showed me her burned hands.
My brother showed me a difficult book.
These were their gifts; the rest was talk.

I discovered my body in the dark.
It had a surprise in its little crack.
I started to say what I'd found in the dark,
but my mother gave me a dirty look
and my father turned a key in the lock.

I was left alone with the difficult book
and the stove that burned my grandmother's hands,
and while they muttered behind my back
I learned to read and to make my bread,
to eat my words and lie flat in my bed.

They took me to school where I learned to be cute;
I wore clean jumpers and washed my hands;
I put my hands up to cover my mouth;
I listened to everything everyone said
and kept what I could in my stuffed-up head.

I had weeping eyes and a chest that coughed,
a stomach that hurt, and a mouth that laughed
whether or not I felt good or bad.
I was always promoted to the next grade.
I graduated; I got laid.

I did what girls were supposed to do.
I wore a white dress; I was photographed;
my teeth were perfect, my knees were crossed.
I cleaned up the mess that the baby made.
I hope that my body's price is paid.

I'm giving the gifts back, one by one.
I'm tearing the pages of my past.
I'm turning my back. I'm turning them down,
I'm burning their strict house to the ground.
May I never want bread at their table again.

May I let go of these bitter rhymes;
and may this burial be my last
while I live in my body and learn from my bones
to make some less predictable sound.
Let this coffin of verses inherit my pain.

SECRET SONG

How can I tell you I've been
stealing. Stole from you.
Hid memories in my skin
of what we did, we do.

Your mouth, my sibling mouth
were printing histories
of children without milk,
predictions of a drought

and long winters in exile —
my poems all the heat, my smile
a code for hurt, a lie
I told you, learning how to spy.

How can I tell you I've been
spying. Looked at you
as you lay sleeping, blue
jacket by my bed, sin

our dead religion — there's no sin
but shame, shame, for shame
I touched you; from your skin
I stole my photo, papers, name.

HOUSEWORK

for M. W.

Through this window, thin rivers
glaze a steep roof. Rain: a church of rain,
a sky—opaque pearl,
branches gemmed with rain,
houses made of rain.

I am in the kitchen
killing flies against the cabinets
with a rolled-up magazine,
no Buddhist—
I live by insisting on my hatreds.

I hate these flies.
With a restless wounding buzz
they settle on the fruit,
the wall—again, again
invading my house of rain.

Their feelers, like hard black hairs,
test the air, or my gaze.
I find I am praying
Stand still for me.
I'll devil the life out of you.

The human swarm comes in
with wet leaves on their sticky boots.
they settle on me with their needs; I am not nice.
Outside, headlights of dark cars are winding the street.
The mirror over the sink will do me in.

At five o'clock, rain done with, in darkness
the houses gather. In the livingrooms
Batman bluely flickers; the children all shut up,
all but an angry baby or a husband.
The suburb is wreathed in wet leaves.

I forget what I wanted. Was it old music
laying gold-leaf on the evening?
Lamplight sweetening the carpet
like honey from Crete: a dream of/door to Egypt?
Something to do with the life force.

December turns the sky to metal,
the leaves to gutter-paper.
Leak stopped, the bedroom ceiling starts to dry.
Its skin of paint is split and curling downward.
There is a fly in this house that will not die.

SONG

for female voices

Suddenly nothing is coming right.
My lovely child has become fat.
Her face is red with ugly scabs.
Love, does it mean I am a bad

        Mummy, please stay with me.
        Don't go to work today.
        My tummy hurts. I want
        milk in my bottle. I want

mother? I wanted to be a great
authoress. Or author's mistress—
I am always late to work. Always
I wanted to be a perfect woman,

        you to lie down with me.
        I peed again in bed—
        my daddy never yells.
        Now you're making me cry.

a mother, big, with wonderful dinners
in the pot, and children I only sing to,
a woman woven of different threads;
flat in the kitchen, but in bed

        I only want my daddy.
        Can't he take care of me?
        He calls me his little
        baby and tucks me in.

I'll play a lute of long hair
and little nightgown; I'll move
like a soft-coated animal; the moon
will be drawn to touch my body in love.

        I want my blanket. Please,
        can't we go to the zoo?
        When I'm big I'll get real babies.
        Then I'll be just like you.

STORY

Once, I took a mouth
into my kitchen —
a little, pretty one,
but it got bigger
in the warm room
and filled my whole
house up. It got
loud then, and its big lips
were fringed with black hair.

It ate out of my hand.
It made me cry.
It made me come.
But what disgusting noises —
I came to hate it.
It fastened on my tit
and would not let
me alone. I loathed
the sound of it sucking.

I had to hack it off,
finally, with a knife,
also to cut off part
of my body: I became
hideous. the lips bled,
and where the drops fell
in the kitchen, the bedroom,
there budded up
hundreds of baby mouths.

WORK SONG

I have been sitting
on this one's lap
a long time, fingering
his gray business
suit: a long time,
smelling the piss
in its sour threads.

He smokes. He smiles
as he strokes my breasts.
I concentrate on hairs,
on cuffs, the red
gleam of his ring.
His thing is stiff.
He licks his lip.

Dear uncledaddy,
tell me how you like
your kitten, your silk mesh,
your anything —
let me know when
you're ready,
what you'll give me.

He gives me what
I ask for, he says
I have it pretty easy.
But I'm tired.
I've been sitting
on this one now
for a long time.

THE WOMEN'S SCHOOL

She wears a pale frown and a tie,
keys at her boy-hip.
Her fingers, like thin lily wands,
curve around a cup.

In my distance: her bony nose
and wild crown of black hair.
The rest are dancing—raucous, but cut off.
No one invited me here,

and they know one another.
"Mitzi" is the name of the dark beauty.
I ask just as she's leaving.
Here we are first names only.

Hot rain from the coffeepot, stained napkins,
spilled wine—my drunken repetitions.
I drink black and maroon potions,
and spill everything.

Everything I was, or wanted. Doll sawdust
spilled on the beat-up floors of the brownstone,
I'm dancing my awkward body among women.
One screams, *Please! Why can't you leave me alone.*

8th Street: The Aquarium

Once, the day white as a jet of whale-spume,
I took the M train on its blowy trestle.

The big open tanks at Brighton
glittered like walls of water.

There were whales,
white and serious behind aquarium glass,

their coupling not for our witness,
but two whose long, slightly stirring bodies

lay in the clear water
magnetically close,

one under the other,
not touching —

hour after hour,
winter sunlight marbling the cold water.

Direct Address

for S. T.

You said,
"I am afraid
I want to be a woman" —

I think it only fair to warn you
it is not what you think
trailing your skirts,
brow-pencil, night cream —
these aren't the feminine
or any softnesses you were denied
but some extreme costume of the heart.
Steve, you wanted to be a queen.

I think it only fair to warn you
the heart is sexless.
It lies undressed in the dark,
and under the silk
or the single earring of gold,
the many-sexed apparel,
the heart, naked, is beating
need   need   need

Song of What I Wanted

I wanted to use your body
for a lock on my light household,
a weight on my shaky table,
an initial in my linen.

I wanted to keep you lying
in a bed where I could find you
deep in a dream of money
and women like plush caves.

With your hair like ancient music
and your eyes like light rockets
I wanted to tie up your laughter
and photograph my scars.

I wanted to keep you needing
me like cool hands on a fever.
And then I wanted to leave you
in the blanket-rags of my absence.

THE FIRE

What I loved about you
finally I have forgotten

It was something to do
with your hair
and the late afternoon
light   the floor
the molten stripe in the table

Nothing had weight or number
coins   apricots   windows
everything burning

and not forgotten
so much as fallen
like a husk   shining   paper
from the burnt grain

SOME UNSAID THINGS

I was not going to say
how you lay with me

nor where your hands went
& left their light impressions

nor whose face was white
as a splash of moonlight

nor who spilled the wine
nor whose blood stained the sheet

nor which one of us wept
to set the dark bed rocking

nor what I took you for
nor what you took me for

nor how your fingertips
in me were roots

light roots torn leaves put down —
nor what you tore from me

nor what confusion came
of our twin names

nor will I say whose body
opened, sucked, whispered

like the ocean, unbalancing
what had seemed a safe position

STOP

I hate it when you
fill my glass up
without asking me.

I always liked
a little
on a plate
in a cup

an egg
with space around it
an orange
with a knife
next to it

a cup
with space above
the coffee

discrete colors
orange pewter black

the porcelain glaze on the china
the blue napkin.

I want to keep things
separate. I hate it
when you break my egg.
I hate when you salt things
when you assume
I want cream

or the shade down
or touch, or looks
of kindness.

I want nothing
to lose
its cutting edge
nothing
to run together.

You had better
stop
pouring yourself
into my glass.

"Vagina" Sonnet

Is "vagina" suitable for use
in a sonnet? I don't suppose so.
a famous poet told me, "Vagina's ugly."
Meaning of course, the *sound* of it. In poems.
Meanwhile, he inserts his penis frequently
into his verse, calling it, seriously, "My
Penis." It is short, I know, and dignified.
I mean of course the sound of it. In poems.
This whole thing is unfortunate, but petty,
like my hangup concerning English Dept. memos
headed "Mr./Mrs./Miss"—only a fishbone
in the throat of the revolution—
a waste of brains—to be concerned about
this minor issue of my cunt's good name.

THE BOMBED VILLAGES

Trees and brown patches
of field broken by a solitary figure
bending
where the house stood, scraping
for children, reedy voices. The room dangles
a patient picture.

You came into it
a stranger. The words were not
your language, nor the hat
a comfortable thing. The trousers —
your hands were not concerned
in the weaving. You dropped
the picture. And
we can move covered
through it, through
the homes dangling, and the smells
not come in, of animals,
shadows of children. As if there were something
certain, our words above all
those shadows, our words refuse
to touch the bricks they pick among.

What singing
comes through the shadows? Hide yourself
in your language, as if the rooms were not
dangling, and the children,
the shadows, the animals
not come through the night
to us. There is a brief illumination
of burned
bridges. Who

will remember
the road back. When rain falls on the rubbish
of broken huts and the air was
dead language.

I am someone else
you say, but the burden of
the woman by the mill, crying
nothing that was not burned here.

NOTES:

"In Western Massachusetts, Sixteen Months Sober": The epigraph is from the soundtrack of Perry Miller's film celebrating the life and work of Georgia O'Keeffe.

"Three Songs after Anna Akhmatova":   In lieu of "literals," I compared diverse English translations by Judith Hemschemeyer, Stanley Kunitz, and D.M. Thomas, and created new versions.

Acknowledgments

Of the previous collections from which many of these poems are reprinted, *Housework* was published in 1975 by the women's independent press Out & Out Books and printed in Brooklyn at The Print Center; *A Long Sound* was published in 1986 by Beatrix Gates' Granite Press; *Cold River* was published in 1997 by Bill Sullivan's Painted Leaf Press.

I am grateful to the editors of periodicals and anthologies in which previously uncollected poems first appeared, some in earlier versions:

Belladonna: A Black Machine Rose, Solo
Columbia Poetry Review: Jew in Paris, Burial, Last Seen, Houston to Tucson, Phoning My Brother
Court Green: Backyard, Ashes, Preview, Tough-Love Muse
5 AM: It
The Gay and Lesbian Review: The Combination
Hanging Loose: Across the Table, Storyville, Virage
Love Speaks its Name: Breathing You In
Lumina: Apprentice
Margie: Testimony
MiPOesias: Triolet: Nutritional Drink; Bethlehem; Bracelet
Natural Bridge: Afterlife, A Garden
Nightsun: Inaugural; Rouen, 1431
Poets as World Witnesses: Kitchen Scene
Washington Square: Processional
Wet: A Journal of Proper Bathing: The Bird, The Offering, The Mask, Heart

Indispensable communities of poetry and friendship helped make this book possible, especially Anne-Marie Macari, Gerald Stern, and the poetry community at New England College to which they first introduced me; The MacDowell Colony, where I completed a draft of this collection; and Donna Brook, Bob Hershon, Marie Carter, Dick Lourie, and all at Hanging Loose Press for their vision, labor, and tireless good humor.

I'm indebted to friends and mentors who read and commented on these poems as they were written: Jean Valentine, Anne Marie Macari, Jan Clausen, Beatrix Gates, Elena Georgiou, Griffin Hansbury, Carl Morse, David Trinidad, and Steve Turtell. Special thanks to Naomi Bushman, Kathleen Culver, Fletcher Copp, Martin Desht, John Masterson, Eileen Myles, and Stanley Siegel. And, always, Kate.